Viviane Barrozo Manfré
Andreia Cristiane Silva Wiezzel

Aggression in early childhood education

Viviane Barrozo Manfré
Andreia Cristiane Silva Wiezzel

Aggression in early childhood education

A study based on Winnicott's Theory

ScienciaScripts

Imprint

Cover image: www.ingimage.com

This book is a translation from the original published under ISBN 978-613-9-73437-5.

Publisher:
Sciencia Scripts
is a trademark of
Dodo Books Indian Ocean Ltd. and OmniScriptum S.R.L publishing group

120 High Road, East Finchley, London, N2 9ED, United Kingdom
Str. Armeneasca 28/1, office 1, Chisinau MD-2012, Republic of Moldova, Europe
Printed at: see last page
ISBN: 978-620-6-21128-0

I dedicate this work to my family, who have always been present at all times of my life, who, with much love, affection and constant support, have spared no effort for me to reach the present stage. To all of you my eternal gratitude and all the love in the world.

Viviane

I dedicate this work to the children who - for various reasons - cannot fully live their childhood, in the certainty of the existence of human resources that can leave them free to grow up. Andreia

SUMMARY

PRESENTATION

This book is the result of a research financed by the National Research Council (CNPq), through which the issue of child aggressiveness was investigated.

The subject has generated concern at world level, which mobilised the researchers to understand the phenomenon and seek ways of helping the child within a public school in São Paulo.

The general objective of the research was to investigate the possible causes of aggressive manifestations of a child in a child education school and to perform an intervention in order to contribute to the quality of his/her interpersonal relationships. To do so, it had as specific objectives: 1 - to identify the relationship difficulties presented by the child; 2 - to reconstruct her life story; and 3 - to provide the child with moments of shelter, expression and possible conflict elaboration through play.

The method used was qualitative research, with the contribution of psychoanalysis, especially the theoretical framework of Winnicott. As instruments of data collection, interviews with the teacher and parents, participant observation and playful activities with the child were used. The data were analyzed from the choice of toys, ways of handling them and verbalizations of the child.

From the analysis of the data collected and the theory studied, it can be concluded that João found in play the possibility of working on feelings and conflicts, repeating everyday situations in play, working with data from reality and fantasy, and also having fun.

The work is organized as follows: in the first part the reader will find all the theoretical reference about aggressiveness and, in the second, the presentation of all the work done with the child and the results obtained. Finally, in the Final Considerations, the authors discuss the reasons for the aggressive manifestations and the importance of parents and teachers knowing and acting in a way that welcomes the child and contributes to its emotional development.

We hope that the reflections presented in this work contribute to the educational professionals, in order to guide their teaching practices, aiming at developing a quality educational practice, understanding, respecting and guiding children.

In the case of any individual at the beginning of the emotional development process, there are three things: at one end there is heredity; at the other end there is the environment that supports or fails and traumatises; and in the middle is the individual living, defending and growing (WINNICOTT, 1983).

INTRODUCTION

Increasingly, there are frequent complaints from professionals in early childhood education about children who present aggressive manifestations in the classroom, interfering in their learning or in that of the group. It is a subject that is difficult to be investigated and worked on, as it presents many variables to be considered and understood.

The understanding of the phenomena that encompass the aggressive manifestations requires the knowledge of human emotional development, since aggressiveness can be manifested in various ways and at various stages of the subject's development.

The aggressive manifestations, characterised as difficulties in relationships, may be related to the experience and living of each child, or also involve strictly internal phenomena which are related to pathologies.

Many authors set out to seek definitions for aggressive manifestations, in an attempt to clarify them. Among them, there are those who followed the psychoanalytic bias, discussing this phenomenon in the development of the child from an early age.

Baggio (1985) points out that aggressiveness is an important phenomenon to be studied and understood, because for him:

> It is obvious that aggressive behaviour represents a problem of extreme gravity and importance for humanity. With the progressive increase in recent decades of the instruments of destruction, with the circumstances of urban life and overpopulation in large cities, man's destructive potential has become even more dangerous. We consider, therefore, this theme as one of the most important to be treated by Developmental Psychology, because it is of crucial importance for the very survival of the human species that the mechanisms by which aggression is acquired and maintained be understood, so that it can be controlled. (BIAGGIO, 1985, p. 153).

For the author, defining aggressiveness is a problem. In an attempt to find a definition, he resorted to authors such as Dollard, Doob, Miller, Mowrer and Sears (1939, apud BAGGIO 1985, p. 153): "Aggression is any sequence of behaviour, the aim of which is to cause harm to the person to whom it is directed". From this definition, it is understood that aggressiveness is intrinsically associated with the action of causing damage.

Baggio (1985) explains that instrumental aggression has received few studies and emphasis, but points out that if this type of aggression is not studied, any act in a war, for example, may be considered instrumental and non-violent, or in fact aggressive. According to the author, hostile aggression can be understood as a tool that results in the suffering of another.

According to Freud (1997, p. 81), "[...] the inclination to aggression constitutes in man an original and self-subsistent instinctive disposition, and I return to my opinion that it is the greatest impediment to civilization". In view of the foregoing, it is understood that, for the author, the obstacle to civilization lies in the fact that all human beings possess an aggressive and hostile instinct towards all and all towards each. "This aggressive instinct is the derivative and the main representative of the death instinct [...]" (FREUD, 1997, p. 81).

According to the author, human beings have two instincts: the life instinct and the death instinct. The latter, in turn, can become destructive when externalised to objects. From this externalised destruction, the subject manages to find a beneficial relief for his organism.

Winnicott, in his works, was dedicated to the study and understanding of aggressiveness and destructiveness, inherent aspects of human nature. According to the author, the central idea in studying aggressiveness consists in the fact that, if society lives in danger, this danger does not stem from aggressiveness itself, but from its repression. For the author, aggressiveness is related to primitive love, as well as its forms of expression.

Aggressiveness is not conceived as something bad or necessarily pathological, since it constitutes a necessary force for the adaptive processes of the human being. According to Winnicott (1982), when the initial phases of emotional development occur well, aggressiveness can become a source of energy to carry out various works such as art, play, study etc.

According to the author:

> It may be that one child tends towards aggressiveness and another hardly reveals any symptoms of aggressiveness from the beginning, although both have the same problem. It simply happens that these two children are dealing in different ways with their loads of aggressive impulses (WINNICOTT, 2005, p. 103).

Based on the conception, in the organization of its internal world, the child tries to keep what it feels as benign, but there are moments when it feels it is necessary to externalize something bad, aiming to eliminate it. This is a phenomenon inherent to the human being and is experienced by the child from an early age, in its relationship with its mother. The movements of babies still in their mothers' bellies cannot be considered as aggressiveness. Until then, it is a motor activity, in which the child is moving and, suddenly, is faced with something: the mother's belly. It should be noted that aggressiveness "is hidden, disguised, diverted, attributed to external agents, and when it manifests itself it is always a difficult task to identify its origins" (WINNICOTT, 2005, p.94).

From a Winnicottian perspective, aggressiveness is understood as a factor inherent to the human being, a natural movement to expose his thoughts and desires, and is also configured as a form of learning about the knowledge of the real world. Therefore, aggressiveness is necessary for the child to adapt and acquire security in the beginning of its life.

Aggression besides being a mechanism for the individual's energy source, collaborates to the baby's perception of external reality, that is, the establishment of what "is the self" and what "is not the self", from very early on. "Aggression is always linked, in this way, to the establishment of a distinction between what is and what is not the self." (WINNICOTT, 2005, p. 104)

Children who show aggressive manifestations have some behavioural characteristics, namely: they do not obey the social rules in the context in which they are inserted (for example, at home, at school, among other places); they have low tolerance to frustration, have frequent angry outbursts, do not obey their parents, have difficulties in interacting socially, in some cases, they fail at school, attack their schoolmates, parents and teachers (physically and/or verbally). They also end up being avoided by their peers out of fear, which increases their discomfort and social exclusion.

After the brief presentation of what aggressiveness is, this paper adopted the assumptions of Winnicott's theory to support the research presented here with a child in early childhood education.

CHAPTER 1

WINNICOTT AND THE STUDIES ON AGGRESSIVENESS

As reported in the work Deprivation and Delinquency (2005), Donald Woods Winnicott (07/04/1896 - 25/01/1971) was a pediatrician and psychoanalyst, exercising his professional activity in clinics and hospitals, and in the context of private practice, the children were taken by their parents and/or guardians to be consulted. At the beginning of his professional experience, Winnicott always avoided attending children who were considered delinquents, due to the fact that he did not feel prepared for such situations and also due to the absence of resources in the hospital to work with these cases. He believed that before attending delinquent children who needed much more than a mere clinical assistance, he should acquire experience in attending common children and parents, in the family and local environment.

However, when the Second World War broke out, it was impossible for Winnicott to avoid delinquency cases, since now the time had come to delve into new experiences beyond those he had acquired in the clinic. Facing the challenges of delinquency, having the responsibility of attending to individual cases, Winnicott took on the Evacuation Consultancy, being appointed as Consultant Psychiatrist of the Government Evacuation Plan, in an institution located in England. The children attended by Winnicott were those who could no longer stay in their ordinary homes - in face of the intolerable situations they were going through - even before the war. Therefore, in some cases, perhaps the war had brought benefits to these children, by providing them with help and relief.

In this context, Winnicott had to face the problems resulting from family disintegration, experiencing the effects of loss: separation, destruction and death. In an attempt to understand the personal reactions and delinquent behaviour of the children, he worked with a local team and, since these children had nowhere else to go, the central concern turned to how to maintain and help them.

This team was composed of a psychiatrist, a social worker and administrators of the homes (there were five homes in all) for children who were considered too disturbed to be placed in ordinary family homes. Winnicott visited the homes once a week. The other members of the team, experienced the impacts of the children's confusion and despair, resulting from behavioural problems. Winnicott, when visiting the homes weekly, carefully recorded the situation of each child and the stress caused to the team members. During the visits, Winnicott would discuss the cases with the team members and what had been done. After such discussions, Winnicott and Clare Winnicott (Winnicott's social worker and sister) would try to come to a conclusion about what was happening, culminating in some temporary theories.

The work with delinquent children, made possible by the war experience, influenced Winnicott's concepts of emotional growth and development; consequently, his theories on antisocial tendency began to emerge. Members of the Evacuation Advisory Board, administrators of the sites, public agencies involved, and the children's parents were often informed about the effect of separation and loss on the children, and also how the institutions were developing in the task of helping them. Winnicott was the main person in this project, because he put it into practice and made it work, bringing together and articulating the experiences of all the members of the team, attributing meanings, offering support and help to these members to maintain their emotional stability in the living with the delinquent children, over an increasingly extended period.

Despite the context in which they were produced, the knowledge obtained from such an experience can be applied to general cases, since the problems resulting from deprivation and delinquency are evident in any circumstance and in a predictable way. Winnicott stresses the importance of an environment that is good, humane and strong enough to contain the aggressiveness of antisocial/delinquent children in need of care.

Winnicott (1982) emphasises that the basis for a healthy emotional development is the maternal bond. For babies to grow and become secure, independent and healthy adults, it is important to ensure a good initial experience, through the love between the mother and her baby, and this relationship begins in the womb.

Therefore, it becomes fundamental for the mother to believe in herself, needing only the technical help of medicine, since the baby needs everything she does naturally, carefree and dedicated to her mission of being a mother. The first form of love that the baby can recognise, therefore, is the mother's physical care for him.

According to Winnicott (1982), the baby has fantasies associated with excitement and feeding. The act of breastfeeding is permeated by aggressive and destructive elements. When the child is excited, in his fantasies, he attacks the mother's body and the maternal breast, not realizing that the body he is attacking is the same body he enjoys when he is calm. Such aggressiveness is associated with the act of feeding and survival, there is no intention of destroying. Thus, initially "there is a theoretical voracity of love or appetite-primary love" (WINNICOTT, 2005, p. 97). In this case, love refers to love-mouth.

Winnicott (1982) emphasises the importance of the mother surviving the baby's attacks:

> The fact that she remains a living person in the baby's life makes it possible for the child to discover that innate sense of guilt which constitutes the only appreciable feeling of guilt and the main source of the urgent impulse to mend, to recreate and to give. There is a natural sequence of relentless love, aggressive attack, feeling of guilt, sense of worry, sadness, desire to correct or mend, to build and to give; this sequence is the essential experience of childhood in its earliest stages, but it cannot become a concrete thing if the mother, or whoever performs her functions for her, cannot live with the child through all these phases and thus make possible the integration of the various elements. (WINNICOTT, 1982, p. 123).

The baby's growth and development occurs gradually. It is up to the mother to provide the appropriate environment for this development to occur in the best possible way. All the baby's physical aspects will be fine if his emotional development is occurring naturally.

Winnicott (1982) uses the term "good enough mother" to refer to the mother who adequately adapts to the needs of her child, since the child thinks it has dominion over external objects (something extremely necessary in the beginning of its life) due to this satisfactory adaptation of the mother. The basis for the child to accept external reality is for the mother to obey it, meeting its needs. Therefore, the child's desires and expectations are met thanks to a world constituted by maternal care, until, little by little, the child can be disillusioned.

For Winnicott (2005), human relations are established from two essential aspects: love and hate. Since the baby's birth, these elements are intensely present in the intimate of the human being. Among the human tendencies, the aggressive manifestations are the most difficult to identify their origins, since, most of the time, aggressiveness is attributed to external factors, being deviated to other activities, remaining camouflaged.

It is fundamental for the child's development that he experiences primary aggressiveness in a phase in which he doesn't necessarily need to feel regret, so that better and more solid bases for his mental health can be established. Aggressiveness is experienced by the child in a very intense way in the first years of life. When manifesting aggressiveness, the child has no idea of the reasons and therefore becomes anguished, considering that intense and contradictory forces are acting in his unconscious.

> [...] when cruel or destructive forces threaten to overwhelm the forces of love, the individual has to do something to save himself, and one of the things he does is to put out his inner self, to dramatize the inner world outwardly, to play the destructive role himself and bring it under control by an external authority (WINNICOTT, 2005, p. 99).

In order for the child to achieve an equilibrium, she therefore needs the help of her caregivers, because there are situations in which "it is the adult's task to prevent this aggression from getting out of control by providing a confident authority within whose limits a certain degree of mischief can be dramatized and enjoyed without danger". (WINNICOTT, 2005, p. 101)

In this context, the child needs to find a way to manifest aggressiveness without causing real harm, that is, without destroying and/or hurting the other. Gradually, as development proceeds, the child's ability to take responsibility for his actions emerges, putting himself in the other's place, not wanting to hurt him.

For Winnicott (2005):

> [...] every aggression that is not denied, and for which personal responsibility can be accepted, is usable to give strength to the work of repair and restitution. Behind all play, work and art is unconscious remorse for the damage done in unconscious fantasy, and an unconscious desire to begin to put things right.(WINNICOTT, 2005, p. 101).

For Winnicott (1982, p. 36) the relationships that the child establishes with other people will be successful if he succeeds in the initial relationship with his mother as a baby: "[...] the only authentic basis for a child's relationships with his mother and father, with other children, and finally with society, consists in the first successful relationship between the mother and the baby [...]"

Winnicott (1982) advises:

> If children need a good, normal home with which to identify, they also deeply need a stable home and a stable emotional environment in which they can have the opportunity to make steady, natural progress in due course during the early stages of development. [...] parental love is not simply a natural instinct they retain within themselves, but something a child absolutely needs to be given. (WINNICOTT, 1982, p. 118).

The satisfactory experiences arising from an emotionally stable home are fundamental for the child to acquire the capacity to get involved with people and also to take responsibility for the aggressive elements, which are inherent to its nature.

Winnicott (2005) states that when there is absence or deficient participation of the mother in the child's early stages of development, the gradual changes in their development will occur in a sudden and unpredictable way.

> By sensitively accompanying the child through this vital phase of early development, the mother will be giving the child time to acquire all the ways of coping with the shock of recognizing the existence of a world outside her magical control. Given time for the maturation processes, the child will become capable of being destructive and of hating, hitting and screaming, instead of magically annihilating the world (WINNICOTT, 2005, p. 109).

Winnicott (2005) explains that the initial stages of emotional development are marked by several conflicts. The child will develop several tests in his home, aiming to disorganize it, especially if he has any doubts about the stability of the environment and its relatives. The child will calm down and play if the home can support everything he does. With this, he will be aware "[...] of a frame of reference if he wants to feel free and if he wants to be able to play, to make his own drawings, to be an irresponsible child". (WINNICOTT, 2005, p. 129).

The child who has not had satisfactory experiences, arising from a stable environment, will not have a frame of reference. Generally, he tends to be anguished, seeking security elsewhere when he still has hopes, that is, he looks for stability and external control, resorting to other family members, friends and school.

As Winnicott (2005) highlights, as a result of environmental failure, the antisocial tendency emerges. This tendency refers to the deprivation/loss of a good relationship, resulting in suffering and anguish, which alter the process of emotional development. The child had a good start, but, in his perspective, everything he counted on is now missing. In face of this, the tendency is characterized as an attempt to recover and/or rediscover a good enough environment and/or a good enough mother.

Theft, being the main characteristic of the antisocial tendency, is often associated with lying. The child who steals an object does not enjoy it, because he is not looking for it, but for the mother figure and her love, which has been lost.

> [When a child steals sugar, he is looking for the good mother, from whom he has the right to take all the sweetness there is. In fact, this sweetness is the child itself, for it has invented the mother and her sweetness from its own capacity to love, from its own primary creativity, whatever that may be. It also seeks the father, if we may say so, who will protect the mother from his attacks on her, attacks made in the exercise of primitive love. When a child steals away from home, he is still seeking the mother, but seeking her with a greater sense of frustration and needing more and more to find, at the same time, the paternal authority that can put a limit on the concrete effect of his impulsive behavior and on the action of the ideas that occur to him when he is excited (WINNICOTT, 2005, p. 131).

Once pointed out some general aspects that involve aggressiveness for Winnicott, some considerations regarding the aggressive manifestations in the school context will be found.

CHAPTER 2

THE MANIFESTATION OF AGGRESSIVENESS AT SCHOOL

The National Curricular Guidelines for Basic Education (BRASIL, 2010, p. 7), when it comes to the reception of children at school, presents the following conception:

> Children come from different and unique socio-cultural, socio-economic and ethnic backgrounds, so they should have the opportunity to be welcomed and respected by the school and by education professionals, based on the principles of individuality, equality, freedom, diversity and plurality.

In view of the above, it is verified that the school institutions receive a diversity of children, with very peculiar characteristics. From this heterogeneity arise demands of various types in the classroom, which requires educators to have the ability to understand and work with these children.

Early childhood education, whose main objective is the integral development of the child, is configured as an important context of socialization, since the child, theoretically, leaves the primary family nucleus and starts to relate to the school group. At this moment, the child may experience relationship difficulties in the classroom, including aggressiveness.

Aggressiveness usually causes apprehension in people who are around the child, either in the family or in school institutions, generating countless controversial discussions on how to deal with its manifestations. The school of child education is faced daily with cases in which children, each time smaller, present exaggerated manifestations of aggressiveness, demanding a work of greater shelter and guidance.

According to Winnicott (2005), difficulties related to aggressiveness are most of the times related to emotional aspects, which leads the child to look for forms of help in the school environment, using, for this, aggressive manifestations so that people help him to resume his emotional development.

As already mentioned, Winnicott (1982, 2005) asserts that a good emotional development of the child results from satisfactory experiences supported in a sufficiently good environment. The destructive impulses become sources of energy, for the realization of activities (work, art, play, etc.), without the child losing the ability to manifest aggressiveness at necessary moments.

If there is any failure in this process, the child may develop some emotional difficulties, characterized by shyness, aggressiveness and even antisocial tendencies. Therefore, if the environment in which the child lives is not stable and facilitating, this may be reflected in his/her behaviour at school.

Winnicott (2005) explains that, in a case of separation of child and mother, the smaller the child is, the more severe the consequences and several feelings will be intensely aroused, because its capacity to keep alive the memory of someone is smaller, and it is easy to forget the person, if it does not see him/her in a certain period of time. In this period of development, the separation from the mother and the child is difficult, causing several symptoms in the child, as well as a very strong feeling of hatred and, at the same time, guilt, since when he felt hatred, he didn't have the opportunity to express this feeling. Aiming at a better understanding of the case exemplified by Winnicott (2005, p. 18):

> The investigation showed that it was not easy for Eddie to reunite with his mother, since at the time of their separation he had hated her, not being able to extract from her presence and smile the assurance that she could remain alive and loving despite his hatred.

Nowadays, more and more mothers are invited to be separated from their children for a certain period of time, due to the professional and social demands placed on them, thus having to leave them in the care of other people, be it a relative, friend, nanny or in a school institution.

In his book, Winnicott (2005) mentions an excerpt taken from a monograph written by Dr. Bowlby, whose theme is the effect of separation from home, and specifically from one's own mother, on the emotional development of infants and young children, namely:

> [...] "are not slates from which the past can be erased with a duster or a sponge, but human beings who carry within them their previous experiences and whose behavior in the present is profoundly affected by what happened before". Citing convincing figures, he was able to show how separation can increase the tendency to develop a psychopathic personality (WINNICOTT, 2005, p. 192).

Given the above, it is understood that the parents' forgetfulness, especially the separation from the mother, causes impacts on the child's life that will influence his emotional development. According to Winnicott, (2005, p. 196) "[...] when the home is good enough, it is the most appropriate place for the child to grow and develop". Thus, when studying the emotional development of a particular child, it is important to identify and understand when, at some point, there was a good environment, but it was undone, or even when it never existed. The effects resulting from both cases are easy to recognize, since there may be repressed hatred or loss of the capacity to love. This is why,

> [...] Other defensive organizations are installed in the child's personality. Regression may occur to some earlier phases of emotional development which were more satisfactory than others, or there may be a state of pathological introversion. It is much more common than one might think for a split in the personality to occur. In the simplest form of schism, the child presents a window, or outward-looking half, built on submission and complacency, while the main part of the self, containing all spontaneity, is kept secret and permanently involved in hidden relationships with idealized fantasy objects (WINNICOTT, 2005, p. 199).

When environmental failure occurs, the child becomes anguished, restless and, in case he/she still has hope, will look for home and the relationships that were missing outside the home, aiming to establish a bond of trust with someone, be it a relative, a neighbour or the teacher. The child will always seek help in spaces in which he feels safe and perceives a concern for him.

The *nursery school* is one of these spaces, being conceived by Winnicott (1982) as an extension of the mother, since it shares with her the necessary care of the young child. Therefore, the school needs to establish a good bond with the mothers, aiming at developing a relationship of trust and collaboration.

The teacher will become very important in the child's life, since the child will relive the relationships established at home with the teacher. However, Winnicott (1982) warns that only when the child has had a good start, characterized by a satisfactory environment, the early childhood teacher will be more likely to succeed in her teaching practice. The smaller the child, the greater the need to establish a close relationship with the mother. Once the mother presents the external reality to her child, it is up to the kindergarten teacher to establish and strengthen the bond with the child's family and provide opportunities for the latter's personal relationships.

According to Winnicott (1982), the school unit receives two characteristic groups of students, namely: children who have had satisfactory experiences at home and children who have not had such experiences due to some failures in the family environment. The first group consists of children who can manage the most diverse feelings they have, being internally better structured and more capable of appropriating the benefits of the education provided by the school.

On the other hand, the second group comes to school looking for a stable environment and, based on the developmental needs of each learner, the school needs to meet these demands by providing them with the sense of security and confidence they need.

Facing these situations, it is up to the school to understand that, for some children, the school environment will not be, primarily, a space for teaching and learning, because, according to their developmental needs and emotional difficulties, they will not be able to effectively appropriate the teaching that is being offered to them. In other words, these children will be attending school not to succeed in the teaching and learning process, but to establish satisfactory bonds, which they are not having at home. This means that children are looking for external people to take care of them and help them deal with their internal aspects.

CHAPTER 3

METHODOLOGICAL PROCESS

Qualitative research, according to Bogdan and Biklen (1982 apud LÚDKE; ANDRÉ,1986, p.13), "[...] involves obtaining descriptive data, obtained in direct contact of the researcher with the situation studied, emphasizes the process more than the product and is concerned with portraying the perspective of the participants".

According to Trivinos (1987):

> Qualitative research has the natural environment as the direct source of data and the researcher as the key instrument. [Qualitative research is descriptive. [Meaning is the essential concern in the qualitative approach. [...] In qualitative research, very generally, one follows the same route when conducting an investigation. That is, there is a choice of an issue or problem, a collection and analysis of information. [...] The information that is gathered is usually interpreted and this may give rise to the requirement for further data searches.(TRIVINOS, 1987, p.128- 131).

The richness of qualitative research consists in the fact that, considering the objectives to be achieved, it is proposed to investigate the movement of people and analyse the context in which they are inserted, as they greatly influence their ways of being and feeling. Thus, the emphasis in this methodological approach does not lie on the result, but on the entire process.

A 4-year-old male child from a Municipal School of Child Education in the city of Presidente Prudente - SP took part in the research.

The project was approved by the Research Ethics Committee of FCT - Unesp (Process No. 045860/2014). Parents and teachers involved signed the Informed Consent Form.

The school and its physical structure are shown in the pictures below:

Figure 1 - School frontage
Source: Viviane Barrozo Manfré

Figure 2 - Access to classrooms
Source: Viviane Barrozo Manfré

Figure 3 - Patio
Source: Viviane Barrozo Manfré

Figure 4 - Corridor leading to the Toy Room.
Source: Viviane Barrozo Manfré

Figure 5 - Access ramp to the courtyard and classrooms.

Source: Viviane Barrozo Manfré

The school unit has the following facilities: 5 classrooms, 1 teachers' room, 1 secretary, 1 directorate, 1 covered patio, 1 reading room, 1 park, 4 bathrooms (two male and two female) and 1 canteen.

The Toy Library was installed in the reading room, and this space was revitalised by students from the Pedagogy course, who participated in the

Interpersonal Relationships at School Project, in 2016.

Figure 6 - School playroom

Source: Viviane Barrozo Manfré

Procedure

In the present research, qualitative in nature, observations in the classroom, interviews with parents and teachers of the child involved and playful interventions with the child in the School Playroom were used as instruments for data collection. The playful activities were performed individually, which occurred once a week, lasting approximately one hour, in the second half of 2016 and first half of 2017.

Playing was chosen as a form of intervention, since play is the way children find to communicate their aggressive feelings, conflicts, fears, without retaliation from the environment. By playing, the child deals creatively with external reality, being able to elaborate traumatic situations. According to Winnicott (1975), the child's play takes place in an area between the psychic reality and the external world, in which the child brings to play objects that belong to its external reality, using them in function of something that comes from its internal reality. In function of his fantasies, in play, the child works with external phenomena, giving them meaning and feeling.

> Through play, children express their conflicts and in this way we can reconstruct their past, just as adults do through words. This is convincing proof that play is a way of expressing past and present conflicts

(ABERASTURY, 1992, p. 17).

Play also serves to work on the child's destructiveness: only in play can an object be destroyed and restored, killed and brought back again, clean and dirty, which favours the conquest of ambivalence.

During the playful meetings, two boxes were provided, which contained several common toys such as plastic cars, jigsaw puzzles, wooden house with furniture, small pots, forks, knives and spoons, crayons, crayons, among others, selected according to the age group of the child (ABERSTURY, 1992). The child had the autonomy to choose which game he/she would like to play, as well as the toys he/she would use. The researcher had an attentive look at the toys chosen by the child and the games she played, being sensitive to the feelings and relational difficulties manifested at these moments. The child theatricalized her experiences and impressions, making it possible to know a little about her and to welcome her.

Figure 7 - Toy boxes made available during playful meetings.

Source: Viviane Barrozo Manfré

The data obtained were organised and analysed according to the precepts of qualitative research, in contribution with interpretations based on the psychoanalytic theory of Winnicott.

CHAPTER 4

PRESENTATION AND DISCUSSION OF THE DATA

Characterisation of the subject

The participating child was studying in a Municipal School of Early Childhood Education, located in the municipality of Presidente Prudente - SP. He was 4 years old and, for ethical reasons, was given the fictitious name João.

John was referred to participate in the research by the teacher, who reported excessive manifestations of aggressiveness "with and without cause", which made the child's relationships in the classroom very difficult because it involved shouting and various types of physical and verbal attacks most of the time. The teacher considered him "*agitated, stubborn, persistent, nervous*" and believed that, in an attempt to solve emerging conflicts, he ended up getting involved in fights with classmates. John did not like to be contradicted and sometimes had a "mood swings", in the teacher's words.

According to the teacher's report, João *was "very good" in terms of* cognitive development, but presented many behaviours to be worked on, several of which were related to aggressiveness.

Interview with the mother

In an interview with the mother, she reported that João lived with his parents and that while they were working, it was the paternal grandmother who took care of the boy. She also reported that the boy's relationship with her and the grandmother was good, without conflicts, but João was jealous of the father and the father, in turn, "had no patience with his son". The mother also mentioned the son's report that the father did not like him and did not praise him.

She said that at home the child did not present behaviours that could be considered aggressive. According to the mother, the problem was located at school, because at home and in the places they frequented, the boy "did not present conflicts", he related well. When João got nervous and "upset" at home, it was as a consequence of his mother fighting with him or when he asked for something and his request was not granted.

The mother said she could not remember any specific situation that happened to the child or to his family that would have led to the emergence of such behaviour. According to her, it was just the boy's "genius".

When the child behaved aggressively, the mother commented that she would talk to him, explaining that he was "wrong" and the child would answer that he would not behave like that anymore. The mother reiterated that there were no specific situations in which the child's aggressiveness increased, except when there were complaints from the school or when the child wanted something and his request was not met by his parents.

João spent the whole day at school and his grandmother picked him up. When he was at home, the boy behaved well, but only when he was with his mother. João, according to his mother, was jealous of his father, to the point of getting "stuck" to her, saying that he was going to date her and that she should marry him.

The mother also reported that the boy played alone and liked to play with cars, play ball, go to the park, play with dirt and watch cartoons. At school, his relationship with his schoolmates was characterized by fights and disagreements, and when he was with his cousins, the relationship between them was considered good. According to the mother, the child was very happy, however, at school he was more "agitated".

In general, the student's school performance was very good, but there were many complaints regarding his behaviour. He had an easy time learning. The mother also reported that João complained that his friends at school did not play with him.

He also said that the boy slept on the floor of his room, because he did not sleep alone. During the period in which the mother was separated from the father (for a year), she emphasized that the boy slept with her in her room. The mother highlighted some of the boy's attitudes considered difficult to deal with, such as the constant fights and disagreements in the school context.

The mother is characterized as a "nervous, hardworking and nice" person. And the father was considered by her as "hardworking", but "impatient".

At the end of the interview, the mother reported that during the period in which she was separated from her husband, she sought the help of a psychologist for the boy, however, she had only managed to take João once to the clinic.

Interview with the teacher

The teacher characterized John as an intelligent and participatory child. She reported that the boy always wanted to help care for the other children, but acted aggressively. He expressed his feelings through shouting and tantrums. When he felt uncomfortable or, to solve a problem, he would end up shouting, crying and hitting his classmates.

The teacher said that the child related very well with her, showed affection and was affectionate. She said that John often told her what happened in his daily life, because he liked to talk to her. The teacher reiterated that the child related very well with a colleague, who was very close to her. "They talk and get along", since the other children preferred not to approach John to avoid the boy's aggressive behaviors.

For her, João had a variable mood, as there were days when he arrived at school "agitated and irritated", and on others, cheerful. The manifestations

the boy's aggressive behaviour was caused by pulling the hair of classmates, tantrums, shouting, physical and verbal attacks. The teacher said that the mother and the paternal grandmother were "quarrelsome" and had a conflictive relationship with each other. She said that since the parents' separation, the child's behavior had worsened because the teacher constantly felt challenged by João.

She pointed out that the parents' relationship may have made the student depressed and sad, because sometimes the parents separated, sometimes they came back. She noticed, during this instability, that the boy became more "agitated", "irritated", constantly challenging her and even hitting his classmates, the teacher emphasized.

When the child showed aggressiveness, to get around the situation the teacher tried to stimulate dialogue, always directing John in such situations to talk to his classmates or to her. However, the teacher often felt sad because she noticed that sooner or later John would return to his initial behaviors.

The teacher closed the interview by stating that apparently the child liked his mother and paternal grandmother very much, but he did not comment on his father and grandfather. She had noticed that the mother was very affectionate towards John.

Playful encounters at the School Playroom

The reports of the playful encounters with the child will be summarized in tables, approaching the main games performed by the child and, presented in groups, the playful encounters.

Table 1 - Summary of playful meetings (1st to 6th meeting)

Find	Play
1°	• When invited to the Toy Room, the student was curious and insecure; however, he accepted. • He opened the boxes and looked curiously at the toys in them; • I had told stories of Little Red Riding Hood using the

	children's literature books, reiterating the idea that: "*the wolf was going to eat the little granny, trying to swallow the little hat and the granny, look how big the wolf was!*" In another story, which featured a boat, he said he wanted the boat in the picture and would ask his father to buy it. In another book about animals, he said that the researcher *would be the owl and he would be the lion, but the lion was crying because he wanted his mother and that made him angry*; • He played doctor and patient; • It had simulated the application of injection in the researcher's arm; • Barbie doll: I had peeked under her clothes; • Played with the doll "Batmam" present in the toy room; • He had "cut" the wolf's feet from the decoration of the room; • He had "shot" the researcher with a toy; • He had not helped to put the toys away: as the researcher put them in the boxes, the child took them out.
2°	• "Barbie" doll: had lifted her dress, said nothing; • He had played doctor and patient: he had simulated giving an injection to the researcher; • He played with the Batmam doll; • He drew: stone, whale and rainbow; • He had mobilised the little wooden house and stuck his head inside saying he was going to sleep for
	rest, as he had worked hard; • He had run the plastic saw over the researcher's head; • He had not helped put the toys away, but he also did not take them out of the boxes while the researcher was putting them away.
3°	• "Saw off the foot of the wolf from the wall decoration of the Toy Room; • Little Red Riding Hood and Princess Ariel story books; • She played at changing the doll's nappy;

	• He had played hide-and-seek behind the little house of the Three Little Pigs; • It had not helped to put the toys away in the boxes.
4°	- Books: storytelling of Princess Ariel to the researcher, without much verbalisation.
5°	• Puzzle; • He had invited the researcher to play with bowling; • She had asked the researcher to draw a whale and a shark; • He lay with his head inside the little wooden house, without verbalising; • He had played hide and seek, asking the researcher to look for him; • It had not helped to put the toys away in the boxes.
6°	• He had taken all the toys out of the boxes, looking at them one by one, not settling on any one; • He had picked up "Barbie" and said that she looked like the researcher and that his mother wore lipstick, just like "Barbie"; • He had furnished the little wooden house; • Bowling; • She had played with animals, reproducing their sounds theirs; • She had told stories of Princess Ariel and the fish;
	• He played hide and seek again; • Only the researcher had kept the toys.

Source: Viviane Barrozo Manfré; Andreia Cristiane Silva Wiezzel.

Figure 8 - Boxes arouse student curiosity in the 1st meeting.
Source: Viviane Barrozo Manfré

Figure 9 - Exploration of the toy boxes in the 1st meeting.
Source: Viviane Barrozo Manfré

Figure 10 - Inconsistency in play in the 6th meeting.
Source: Viviane Barrozo Manfré

As shown in the table, despite his insecurity about the invitation, at the first meeting, John immediately picked up the toys and was not afraid to open the boxes; at the moment, his curiosity was aroused. João showed himself to be a very communicative child and at certain times he invited the researcher to participate in the games. At first he explored all the toys at once, in a great hurry, just as he did in the classroom. He didn't help the researcher put the toys away because he didn't want to interrupt the activity.

In the second meeting he noticed the image of a wolf - referring to the story of Little Red Riding Hood - on the wall of the library, showing a certain discomfort. Then she took the plastic saw and started to "saw the wolf's feet off", which was her favorite game of the meeting, in which it was possible to let out a lot of aggressiveness. In the game with the little house, he expressed an initial conflict to be investigated, related to the need for "rest". He didn't want to finish the activity, but also didn't try to stop the researcher when putting the toys away.

At the next meeting, the first act in the library was, looking for the image of the wolf. He hid behind the "little house of the three little pigs" (puppet house) to try to throw toys at the wolf. Then he took the plastic saw and simulated to "saw" the researcher's head, without verbalizations. The alternation between play with exploration of toys and expression of feelings and conflicts was also noticeable. In the meeting mentioned, there was no acceptance of the end of the playful activity.

In the fifth meeting, she showed a greater affective closeness to the researcher, when inviting her to participate in a bowling game. She lay down inside the wooden dolls' house, without verbalizing, demonstrating the need to be sheltered. In the following meeting, she went back to the exploration of objects, alternating with the already performed games of expression of feelings. One of the main changes presented by the child was to make direct mention of the mother.

At the beginning of the meetings, João did not want to interrupt the playful activity, however, over time, he was showing that, in addition to playing, he did not intend to interrupt contact with the researcher, but gradually began to accept the rules and help put the toys away.

When he hid behind the "little house of the three little pigs", he expected a shield, a protection so that he could "attack" the wolf. The figure made him feel afraid and he often asked the researcher to hide with him, behind the little house, and before the wolf attacked, he was under the protection of the former. João showed that he wanted to face his inner difficulty and took the initiative. However, he needed a support, which was promptly offered to him. The child lived on the defensive: he attacked whatever he was afraid of.

The alternation between exploration play and expression of feelings can be observed, among other aspects, in the playful encounters below.

Table 2 - Summary of playful meetings (7th to 11th)

Meetings	Play
7°	• He played with the animals, reproducing their sounds; • He had played doctor and patient: he had simulated giving an injection to the researcher; • He had played at furnishing the little house and put his head inside it; • I had played catch.
8°	• He came towards the researcher smiling and hugging her; • I had played hide and seek; • He had played at being a little train, saying that only two people would fit inside: him and the researcher; • He played with "Iron Man"; • He had caught a jaguar, saying that the jaguar was his mother and was attacking a giraffe. • He played with the little train; • He had told stories to the researcher, among the stories told were: Little Red Riding Hood; a story about a boat and another story in which he was a lion who was crying because he wanted his mother

	and was therefore angry; • He had put the toys away in their boxes and agreed to go back to the classroom as if he had done what he was supposed to do: *now we can go back to the classroom* - he said.
9°	• He had taken the initiative to pick up and handle the objects from the boxes; • Interest in books; • Instead of laying his head in the little house that day, he furnished the little house; • She had played at hiding cars in the play dough; • I had played at making soap bubbles and bursting them; • Iron Man;
	• Saw the wall with the plastic saw; • Doctor's instruments: the researcher had been the patient and the child the doctor; • Police car; • Initially the child had refused to help put the toys away.
10°	• Ninja turtle; • *Batmam*; • Iron Man; • Saw; • Soap bubble (asked the researcher burst the bubbles); • Snowman from the film*Frozen*; • He had denoted a tray as a bed and said that: "*The bed is children's and the children and the mummy who sleeps in it*" • Pasta: had asked the researcher for help to open the jars; • He had invited the researcher to make a symbol ; • Soap bubble; • Books; • Shark: *"Look at the shark, he eats fish. shark is trying to get his mother*";

	• Lizard: *"My grandmother has a lizard, Viviane*"; • He had bitten the plastic ball; • He furnished the little house; • *Batmam*; • Iron Man; • He had simulated the noise of a shot and said: "The lizard".
11°	• On the way to the playroom, the child said: *"Viviane, I love you so much!* • Play dough: stack the jars; • Soap bubbles and the researcher bursting them; • The boy had said*: "My mother is called Ariane, this is her bed".*
	• Soap bubble; • Pasta; • Iron Man and B *atmam*; • *"The lizard climbed on top of the house. The house calls the baby's mother. The lizard will sleep on top of the mother's house to rest";* • Pasta; • Soap bubble; • The child will help put the toys away.

Source: Viviane Barrozo Manfré; Andreia Cristiane Silva Wiezzel.

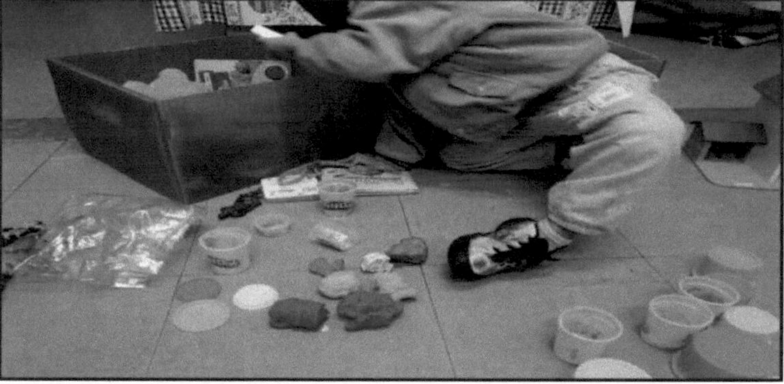

Figure 11 - Playing with play dough on the 9th meeting.
Source: Viviane Barrozo Manfré

Figure 12 - Playing to furnish the little house on the 11th meeting.
Source: Viviane Barrozo Manfré

The games described in the table above, show the alternation between exploration games and expression of feelings, and the boy narrowed even more his interaction and affective contact with the researcher. In the games he theatricalized his ambivalent feelings for his mother, of love and anger, typical of his age.

In addition, the boy explored several books on the shelf in the room, but did not ask for a story to be told. João was also interested in repairing a bridge (built with pieces from the puzzle) with a hammer and furnishing the big wooden house in the library. After the house was "fixed" he would literally stick his head inside and say that he was going to sleep/rest because he had worked hard fixing the bridge.

João, in one of the playful meetings, picked up a toy symbolizing a jaguar and said it was his mother. This would be the tiger, but both would "catch" the other animals. Then he began to represent hostile acts of the jaguar against a giraffe, took an ox (which represented himself) and said that he had killed the jaguar.

The researcher, faced with João's refusal to end the meetings, always reaffirmed that they would play again the following week and, little by little, he began to have confidence that he would return. The child, at this point in his playtime, started to integrate one game with another, for example, he hid some cars inside the play dough and made up stories involving the toys.

João expressed a bond with the researcher, feeling confident when expressing his feelings. In an interview with the child's mother, she stated that she and the child slept in the same bed, just as João had demonstrated in the game with the board.

As the boy handled the books, the researcher observed that he did not do so with the intention of being told stories, but with the intention of telling his own story. He used the books as a tool to have the opportunity to talk about his life, the things he liked and the things he disliked.

Particularly, the stories told by the boy met his fears, fears or fantasy aspects. Through the stories, internal tensions were exposed, which were expressed, initially, through the persecutory image of the wolf, which represented the figure of João's father. Through the evolution of the games, João expressed his conflicts more and more clearly, as in the game mentioned, where he "put" his head inside the little wooden house. This specific play revealed a desire for physical closeness with the mother's body, feeling her absence while he was in the school environment.

Table 3 - Summary of playful meetings (12th to 15th meeting)

Meetings	Play
12°	• Stacks jars of play dough; • The researcher has to burst the bubbles of soap; • Iron Man and Batmam; • Book: just skim; • Hammering toys; • Bury Iron Man and Batman's heads in the play dough; • Bury little cars in the play dough; • The child had said: *"look Viviane, I hurt myself yesterday (I was running and fell)";* • He had invited the researcher to make a

	doughnut cake; • She had picked up the princess crown. The researcher asks, "Who will wear this crown*?" He answers: - You, Viviane."* • *Batmam* and Iron Man; • I had kept only the little doughs.
13°	- Pots of play dough;
	• Iron Man and Batmam; • Pasta; • Board that the child had named decama; • She had taken the play doughs and put them on the bed (tray) to sleep; • He had played doctor; • Cut the dough with plastic scissors; • I had played at ironing the dress of *Little Red Riding Hood*'s puppet; • *I like you very much !";* he told researcher. • I had played aeroplane; • Storybook; • He had taken a plastic lizard and stuck it to the wall with the play dough; • *Little Red Riding Hood* story book (did not want the researcher to tell the story); • Cardboard plane; • It had not helped to put away the toys from the boxes.
14°	• He handled the play dough without verbalising; • Iron Man; • Soap bubbles, asking the researcher to pop them; • Hammering the dough: no verbalization. • Story books: fish, mermaid, witch, whale- tell story to researcher. • I helped her put the toys in the box. I said: It*'s about time, isn't it?*
15°	• Hammering on the dough; • Batman: bury his head in the putty and pull it out

	again.... Head reappears like magic. • He had started to reproduce a situation
	had arrived involving sharks, but not at finalize, he had kept them in the jarspasta himself. • He laid down in the toy box which he emptied. • I had kept only the little doughs.

Source: Viviane Barrozo Manfré; Andreia Cristiane Silva Wiezzel.

Figure 13 - Playing with play dough on the 12th meeting
Source: Viviane Barrozo Manfré

The child began to put the researcher in the position of a queen. The queen, in turn, was equivalent to the mother. João was experiencing with the researcher something that resembled his relationship with his mother, or that he was experiencing, but considered insufficient. When the boy started to put away the dough, he accepted to "win and lose the researcher", because he had already elaborated that the "separation" would be temporary and trusted in her return.

When the child took the plastic lizard and stuck it to the wall with the play dough, it symbolized, again, the desire to have physical contact with the mother's body, and may even be something related to the breastfeeding process. The lizard was João. The fact that he did not help to put away the toys from the boxes that day showed that he was in conflict, once again, with his maternal insecurities. From the moment he managed to establish a bond with the researcher in some maternal aspects, his needs eased and he no longer feared the end of the play dates. João was managing to use play to meet his emotional needs.

Table 4 - Summary of playful meetings (16th to 19th meeting)

Meetings	Play
16°	• Hammering dough; • He furnished the house; • Piling up pots of peanut butter and knocking over the tower; • Making sharks with a signature modelling and kneaded them, squeezed them, destroyed them; • I had made a drawing for the teacher: whale and shark; • When it was time to leave, she only kept the noodles.
17°	• I had made sharks out of play dough; • He piled up the jars of play dough and knocked them over; • Batmam; • Police car; • He had crashed the police car into the pots of pasta; • Child had noticed the missing propeller on the cardboard plane and remembered that it had been the same one that "spoiled" it; • Iron Man killed the jaguar; • I will keep only the dough.
18°	• Pasta; • Batmam; • He verbalised his jokes; • They had assumed that they had started to tuck tail and wings of the paper aeroplane, because he was afraid of the noise.

	• Modelling clay; • Saw; • Hammer; • He started to make noises and asked The researcher closed her ears, because it was a surprise: she squeezed the little rubber fish to make the sound come out, and threw the little plate on the ground. • He had agreed to help, but had not put the toys away and asked if they would play again "tomorrow".
19°	• He played with the doctor's case, without verbalising; he used an injection. • She had made a cake with dough and cut it with a knife, saying that "the biggest piece was for Mum". • He didn't help put the toys away: he asked if he could take them to his friends to play, too, in the classroom.

Source: Viviane Barrozo Manfré; Andreia Cristiane Silva Wiezzel.

Figure 14 - Playing with the police car on the 17th date.
Source: Viviane Barrozo Manfré

Figure 15 - Modelling play dough on the 18th meeting.
Source: Viviane Barrozo Manfré

Among the games, without a doubt, what stood out the most was João's act of taking responsibility for the destruction of parts of the cardboard aeroplane, constituting a first step in the evolution of emotional development and aggressiveness, according to Winnicott (2005). In the meetings, he didn't want to interrupt the activity, he believed to be using the play to solve his conflicts.

In the last playful meeting João baked a cake, saying that the first piece would be his mother's, externalizing an alleviation of his discomfort with her. Also on the same day, and as described in the box, John did not want to keep the toys, because he wanted to share them with his friends. This showed that the boy was wanting to get closer to his friends, to share something good with them.

The qualitative leap in João's interpersonal relationships was noticeable, bearing in mind that when he started the project he used to carry out physical and verbal attacks, shouting and tantrums most of the time he stayed in the institution, which resulted in many complaints about the boy from the teacher, peers and those responsible for his classmates.

After the participation in the project, based on the information obtained by the teacher, the boy changed his way of behaving and reacting in conflict situations, since his relationship with his peers improved a lot, to the point that the complaints eased significantly.

With regard to aggressive manifestations, the teacher also said that these were happening to a lesser extent, in isolated situations, from her perspective as a way of reacting to the provocations of colleagues.

CHAPTER 5

CONCLUDING REMARKS

For Winnicott (2005), aggressiveness is hardly related to a single factor. However, the author always emphasizes the presence of a gap in the child's initial affective relationships marked by ruptures or absences greater than he can bear. As soon as he was born, John stayed for some time being cared for by his mother and was then taken care of by his paternal grandmother, at the age of four he started to attend school full time and was clearly trying to adapt to this new reality.

In the midst of all this, a child with parents in a relationship in crisis, with endings and returns, and a strained relationship between the mother and the paternal grandmother, who has always taken care of the boy. Besides this, because of his age, João is going through the Oedipus Complex, having to live through conflicts inherent to all these situations simultaneously.

In the midst of this process, insecurity, fear, mistrust, love, anger, aggressiveness not yet well-directed, hostility, distrust, guilt, the feeling of being persecuted are justified.

It is understood that the manifestations of aggressiveness in the school environment indicate the presence of factors that have become obstacles for João's emotional development to flow, causing him to react, in search of help and, for some reason, he elected the school for this.

Considering the school as a training space, aiming to ensure the integral development of the student, it ends up influencing directly the subject's training. Winnicott (1982) argues that the child, when entering the school group, still needs care that is very close to maternal care, but warns:

> The school, which is a support but not an alternative to the child's home, may provide opportunities for a deep personal relationship with people other than the parents. These opportunities present themselves in the person of the teacher and the other children and in the establishment of a tolerant but solid framework in which experiences can be held (WINNICOTT, 1982, p.217).

From the analysis of the data and the theory studied, it can be concluded that João found in play the possibility of working out feelings and conflicts he was having, repeating everyday situations in play, working with data from reality and fantasy, and also having fun. Therefore, playing is a privileged activity for emotional development and children need to have opportunities and be encouraged to play at home and at school.

João's play revealed a desire to get closer to his mother, to be cuddled, to be held, to feel accepted by her. João misses his mother and sometimes he was "angry" in class because of this feeling. In the present work only a part of his conflicts were mentioned, which materialize in his interpersonal relationships at school.

As children's language is not yet fully developed, it is up to the school to guide the child about the importance of dialogue and, the teacher, observing more serious conflicts between children, to interfere in order to guide them. Something that does not help children in the development of socialization in this age group is to let them "solve it themselves". Children need to be guided on constructive ways of solving conflicts so that, later on, each one, in his/her own time, can put them into practice.

Through his playing, João felt stronger, more secure, tending to gradually take responsibility for his aggressiveness, supported by the researcher. Throughout the research, John went through several moments in his playing, as follows: 1st moment: playing to release his aggressiveness; 2nd moment: theatrical representation of life issues and the conflicts he was going through; 3ª moment: expressive play and the beginning of conflict elaboration; 4th moment: facing conflicts (play in which he tries to find solutions to conflicts or shows he has already found them) and 5th moment: light play, without the weight of major emotional conflicts.

It should be noted that the moments of João's play were exposed in this way with the objective of making it easier for the reader to understand, which means that we are not implying that the referred moments of João's play are watertight.

Playing was presented as a way of easing the tensions that made the boy manifest aggressiveness in the classroom, a resource that can be used by the teacher to work with the emotional aspects of the child, as well as the guidance:

> [...] the teacher must, at times, protect children from themselves and exercise the necessary control and guidance in the immediate situation; and, in addition, ensure the provision of satisfactory play activities for constructive channels and for acquiring effective skills. (WINNICOTT, 1982, p. 223).

The sooner parents and teachers understand the emotional aspects of children who manifest aggressiveness, the easier it will become to deal with them, both at home and in the school context.

CHAPTER 6

REFERENCES

ABERASTURY, Arminda. **A criança e seus jogos.** 2 ed. Porto Alegre: Artmed, 1992.

BAGGIO, A M. B. **Psicologia do Desenvolvimento**. 8 ed. Petrópolis: Vozes, 1985.

BRASIL. **Resolution CNE/CBE n. 4/2010**. Defines General National Curricular Guidelines for Basic Education. Brasília, 2010.

FREUD, S. **O mal-Estar na civilização**. Rio de Janeiro: Imago, 1997.

LÚDKE, M.; ANDRÉ, M. E. D. A. **Pesquisa em Educação: abordagens qualitativas**. São Paulo: EPU, 1986.

TRIVINOS, A. N. S. Pesquisa qualitativa. In: TRIVINOS, A. N. S. **Introdução à pesquisa em ciências sociais: a pesquisa qualitativa em educação**. São Paulo: Atlas, 1987. p. 116-133.

WINNICOTT, D. W. **The child and his world**. 6 ed. Rio de Janeiro: LTC - Livros Técnicos e Científicos -, 1982.

WINNICOTT, D. W. **Da pediatria à psicanálise**. Rio de Janeiro: Imago, 2000.

WINNICOTT, D. W. **The environment and the maturation processes:** studies on the theory of emotional development. Porto Alegre: Artmed, 1983. p. 125.

WINNICOTT, D. W. **Play and reality**. Rio de Janeiro: Imago, 1975.

WINNICOTT, D. W. **Privação e delinquência**. 4 ed. São Paulo: Martins Fontes, 2005.

ANNEX

FACULDADE DE CIÊNCIAS E
TECNOLOGIA - UNESP/
CAMPUS DE PRESIDENTE

PROOF OF PROJECT SUBMISSION

RESEARCH PROJECT DATA

Research Title: Aggressive and shy children at school: investigation and intervention through the , ludic

Researcher: Andreia Cristiane Silva Wiezzel

Version: 1

CAAE: 31996114.5.0000.5402

Proponent Institution: UNIVERSIDADE ESTADUAL PAULISTA JULIO DE MESQUITA FILHO

VOUCHER DATA

Voucher Number: 045860/2014

Main Sponsor: Self Funding

Endereço: Rua Roberto Simonsen, 305
Bairro: Centro Educacional **CEP:** 19.060-900
UF: SP **Município:** PRESIDENTE PRUDENTE
Telefone: (18)3229-5315 **Fax:** (18)3229-5353 **E-mail:** cep@fct.unesp.br

Printed by Books on Demand GmbH, Norderstedt / Germany